ASD and Me

Learning About High Functioning Autism Spectrum Disorder

West Bend Library

Written and Illustrated by Teresa DeMars
Special Illustration by Donnie DeMars

Charity Press Books

To Donnie: I love you 1,000,000 different ways!

Love, Mom

Part of the proceeds from this book's sales will be donated to various autism charities and school special education programs.

Acknowledgments

I would like to thank the many people who contributed suggestions and reviewed this book's manuscript. They include moms and dads of children on the spectrum, teachers and staff from the Cannon River STEM School and Faribault School District #656, special education specialists from the Minnesota State Department of Education, and autism therapists from Partners In Excellence. I appreciate the time you took to help make this book a reality and your dedication to teaching children with ASD.

Hello! My name is Eli. I live in a brown house at 642
1st Street. I have a mom, a dad, and a little sister named
Emma. My cat likes to sleep on my bed. His name is MJ.

When I was younger, I went to the doctor a lot because I had some special behaviors that made me different from other kids. I could say and read all my letters by the time I was two years old. I liked saying my letters better than talking to my family.

Instead of pretending to drive my toy cars, I liked to line them up all in a row.

I liked to stare at things from all kinds of different angles, and I *really* liked to watch things spin.

The doctor tested me to figure out how my brain worked. He told my parents and me that I have ASD, or Autism Spectrum Disorder. Most people just call it autism. I like calling it ASD.

You can't catch ASD like you can catch a cold. Some doctors think kids are born with ASD. Others think that yucky stuff, like poison, causes it. Doctors are working really hard to find out why kids get ASD.

I used to go to a special school for kids who have ASD. I learned new skills to help me fit in with others. Now I go to a school with all types of boys and girls.

Every kid in the world is different. We can see some of these differences on the *outside* of the body. Some kids have light skin, others have dark skin. Some kids have black or brown hair, others have red or yellow hair. We can see lots of differences.

Other differences are hidden on the *inside* of the body. ASD affects the way the brain works. Because of this, kids like me think about things differently. And ASD can affect kids in different ways. Some kids that have it can't talk at all. Others, like me, can talk a lot.

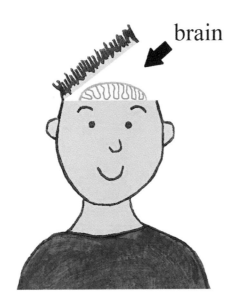

brain

Our differences make each of us special in our own way. How are you different from other kids?

Sometimes I have trouble putting together the right words for what I want to say. People have trouble understanding me. Other times, I do NOT understand what people are saying to me, and that can make me very upset. Does that ever happen to you? It's frustrating!

When I was younger, I didn't know what to say when people said "hello" to me. My friends thought I was ignoring them because I didn't answer back. At my special school I learned how to say "hello" and "goodbye." Now I greet people when I see them.

Sometimes it's hard for me to make new friends. I learned how to ask, "Do you want to play?" Using words makes it easier for me to join in play with other kids.

Other times I just need to be alone. I like to think about baseball and numbers. This helps me gather my thoughts and calm down.

Often I get distracted by things going on around me. I forget to talk to my friends. My teachers and parents remind me to "use my words" and look at my friends when I talk to them.

Because of my ASD, I am very sensitive to the world around me. When there are exciting things or a lot of people around, it gives me so much energy that I just need to SHOW IT! I used to flap my hands like a bird when I got excited about something. I have learned to squeeze my hands together instead.

Loud noises sometimes bother me, so I plug my ears. I really don't like to flush the toilet, but I have learned to do it to keep the toilet clean.

When things around me change, or when things don't go my way, I can get very angry or very sad. Sometimes I just lie down on the ground and cry. I am learning to use words to tell other people how I am feeling. I say, "I am so MAD!" I also take deep breaths and count to ten. Do you ever get mad? How do you calm down?

When I was younger, I thought foods like applesauce and mashed potatoes were yucky. They felt too mushy for me to eat. With help from my mom and teachers at my special school, I learned how to eat these types of foods.

Now I like to eat lots of different fruits and vegetables. Some kids with ASD have special diets. My favorite fruit is watermelon. Mmm, mmm ... I'm HUNGRY!!! What's your favorite food?

It used to be hard for me to color. My fingers had trouble gripping the crayons. It took a lot of practice to write and color. Now I can write letters, numbers, and my name and draw pictures of my family.

Even though I have ASD, I can do all sorts of things. Just like other kids, I like to jump on my trampoline. Do you like to jump? I can jump really, really high!

Just like other kids, I like to swing in my backyard. Last year I learned how to pump, all by myself!

Just like other kids, I like to play baseball. I can hit home runs like the big league ball players. I like to play in the outfield and run around the bases. I collect baseball cards too! Which team do you like best?

At school I like
to read books,

paint pictures,

and play on
the computer,
just like other
kids.

But by far, my most
FAVORITE thing to do,
the BEST thing in the
whole wide world, is
MATH!

I LOVE NUMBERS
AND DOING
MATH!

Did you know
there are 7 colors
in a rainbow?

And there are 12 months in 1 year!

And did you know that 7 + 12 = 19!

5, 10, 15, 20, 25

10, 20, 30, 40, 50

2, 4, 6, 8, 10

My favorite number is 10, but I also like 5 and 15. I love counting by 5's! And 10's! And 2's! Numbers go on … and on … and on!

What's your favorite number?

I love measuring things with a ruler. My cat, MJ, is 15 inches tall! My little sister, Emma, is 38 inches tall, and I am 50 inches tall!

Everywhere I go, I take my calculator with me so I can add and subtract, multiply and divide. Most kids with ASD have a favorite activity that they really LOVE to do. Some kids are super smart in subjects like art, math, reading, music, or science. What's your favorite activity to do?

Aa Bb Cc Dd Ee Ff Gg Hh Ii Jj Kk Ll Mm Nn Oo Pp Qq Rr Ss Tt Uu Vv Ww Xx Yy Zz

You can learn a lot from a kid who has ASD. All you have to do is be their friend.

Dear parents, families, and friends,

You may have heard the public service announcement on the radio from Autism Speaks, which educates listeners about the most common symptoms of autism: "No big smiles or other warm, joyful expressions by six months, no back-and-forth sharing of sounds, smiles, or other facial expressions by nine months, or no babbling by 12 months..."[1]

I remember hearing this radio commercial and thinking to myself, "I'm glad our son doesn't have autism." Our son, Donnie, could do all of those things. He met his milestones, had an advanced vocabulary, and enjoyed being around other kids. Our son did have some quirky behaviors, but we dismissed them because all children say and do funny things. What toddler doesn't like to act goofy and jump around, or act irrational when they don't get their way?

While I wondered why he did some of his "quirky" behaviors, I never imagined that it could be autism. It wasn't until Jenny McCarthy came out in public to tell about her son's autism that I figured out that there was something different about Donnie. In a *People*[2] magazine article, Jenny described the way her son flapped his hands like a bird. Donnie did the same thing when he got excited about something. After I went online to research more about autism, it soon became clear to me that our son fell somewhere on the high end of the spectrum. Shortly before his fourth birthday, our son received the diagnosis of Autism Spectrum Disorder (ASD).

Diagnosing young children with high functioning ASD can sometimes be difficult because they have language and seem like other kids, just quirky. Our son could have been diagnosed at a much earlier age if I had only known about some of the many other symptoms of ASD.

Here are ten more symptoms of Autism Spectrum Disorder:

1. Repeating words or phrases. Some children with ASD will spontaneously repeat words or phrases that they hear someone else say. For example, you are driving in the car with the radio on and a news report comes on talking about "the war in Iraq." A child with this symptom of ASD might spontaneously repeat "the war in Iraq" a few seconds after hearing the radio reporter say the exact same words. This process of repeating words or phrases after hearing them is called echolalia.

2. Self-stimulating behaviors. Also known as "stimming," this behavior occurs when children self-regulate the sensory inputs they are experiencing from the world around them. Examples include hand flapping "like a bird," rocking back and forth or from side to side, looking at things from different angles, spinning around in a circle, twirling their hair between their fingers, making groaning or humming sounds, grinding their teeth, and touching their thumb and fingers together in front of their eyes. These behaviors can occur when the child is exited, bored, or overwhelmed. Stimming helps children with ASD cope with all the sights, sounds, and smells that can make situations stressful for them. Stimming also helps children express the magnitude of excitement they might feel for something.

3. Pronoun confusion. For children with ASD, pronouns can be especially difficult to learn. These words are abstract in nature and can take many months, even more than a year for children with ASD to learn. For example, if you ask, "Do you want a cookie?" a child with ASD might answer, "You want a cookie" instead of "I want a cookie."

---

1   Originally published as *Red Flags* by First Signs, Inc. 2001-2005.
2   Alexander, Bryan. "My Autistic Son: A Story of Hope." *People* 1 Oct. 2007: 120-129.

4. Troubles with transition. Transitioning from one activity to another can sometimes be very difficult for a child with ASD. Leaving play dates, the park, school, or grandma's can cause a major meltdown.

5. Difficulty with imaginative play and thinking. Children with ASD "play" with toys, but in a different way compared with typically developing children. For example, instead of pushing a toy truck around on the ground and saying "vroom, vroom," a child with ASD may line the toy trucks up in a row. It is more fun to organize the toys than to pretend to drive them. Keep in mind that this difficulty may not occur with every toy. A child with high functioning ASD may play as a typical child would with some toys and differently with others. Children with ASD may also struggle to make up a story or describe what is happening in a book or picture. For example, if you showed a typically developing child a picture illustrating the children's nursery rhyme "Mary Had a Little Lamb," the child might say, "There's the little girl who takes the lamb to school and the teacher got mad at her." A child with high functioning ASD might say, "Mary had a little lamb whose fleece was white as snow…" The child would say what he or she had memorized when the story was read to them. Making something up about the picture is very difficult for a child with ASD.

6. Sensitivity to light, sound, and/or touch. The environment around them will often bother children with ASD. Examples include refusing to eat certain foods because of their texture; plugging their ears when hearing loud or new sounds, like the flush of a toilet in a public restroom; constantly taking off socks and shoes or being bothered by clothing tags; and complaining about the sun or florescent lights in large stores. Sometimes, children with ASD will lie on the ground when the surrounding environment overwhelms them.

7. Difficulty sleeping through the night. Children with ASD will often wake up during the night for an hour or two. They have difficulty falling back to sleep because they are wide awake.

8. Fascination with certain objects or subjects. Often, children with ASD will be fascinated with certain objects or subjects to the point where they may seem obsessed. Examples include opening and closing of doors, staring at objects and studying them at different angles, interests in trains, whales, math, rocks, vacuums, wheelchairs… you name it; it can be anything.

9. Hyperlexia. Some children with ASD will exhibit hyperlexia, or the ability to learn numbers, letters, shapes, or words at an earlier age than typically developing children. For example, a typically developing one-and-a-half-year-old would not be interested in or be able to easily learn to read their ABC's or their numbers or be able to identify a pentagon. Hyperlexic children have the ability to learn letters, numbers, and shapes quickly at a very early age.

10. Problems with social skills. Children with high functioning ASD may have problems in social situations. Often they will not respond to a "hello" or "goodbye" and may struggle to make eye contact when talking with another person. Often children with ASD will be unable to ask a peer for a toy or an adult for help when needed. When in group situations, these children may keep to themselves instead of interacting with other children. A child with ASD may have a large vocabulary but may struggle to put the words together to keep a conversation going.

Each child with ASD is completely unique. While there are some similarities between them, each child exhibits a unique combination of symptoms and functions at a different skill level. That's why it can be so hard for a child's primary doctor to diagnose the disorder. If you suspect your child might be on the spectrum, consider taking him or her to a licensed psychologist for a diagnosis. Also, your local school district can evaluate your child and is a great place to start.

For more information, find us on Facebook: http://www.facebook.com/ASDandMe

Made in the USA
Charleston, SC
26 September 2013